Dear Parent:
Your child's love of reading starts here!

Every child learns to read in a different way and at his or her own speed. You can help your young reader improve and become more confident by encouraging his or her own interests and abilities. You can also guide your child's spiritual development by reading stories with biblical values and Bible stories, like I Can Read! books published by Zonderkidz. From books your child reads with you to the first books he or she reads alone, there are I Can Read! books for every stage of reading:

SHARED READING
Basic language, word repetition, and whimsical illustrations, ideal for sharing with your emergent reader.

BEGINNING READING
Short sentences, familiar words, and simple concepts for children eager to read on their own.

READING WITH HELP
Engaging stories, longer sentences, and language play for developing readers.

READING ALONE
Complex plots, challenging vocabulary, and high-interest topics for the independent reader.

ADVANCED READING
Short paragraphs, chapters, and exciting themes for the perfect bridge to chapter books.

I Can Read! books have introduced children to the joy of reading since 1957. Featuring award-winning authors and illustrators and a fabulous cast of beloved characters, I Can Read! books set the standard for beginning readers.

A lifetime of discovery begins with the magical words **"I Can Read!"**

Visit www.icanread.com for information on enriching your child's reading experience.
Visit www.zonderkidz.com for more Zonderkidz I Can Read! titles.

The Lord is my shepherd.
He gives me everything I need.
Psalm 23:1

ZONDERKIDZ

Jesus Feeds the Five Thousand
Copyright © 2011 by Zonderkidz
Illustrations © 2011 by Valerie Sokolova

Requests for information should be addressed to:
Zonderkidz, *Grand Rapids, Michigan 49530*

Library of Congress Cataloging-in-Publication Data

Bowman, Crystal.
    Jesus feeds the five thousand / by Crystal Bowman.
       p. cm.
    Illustrated by Valerie Sokolova.
    ISBN 978-0-310-72157-4 (softcover)
    1. Feeding of the five thousand (Miracle)—Juvenile literature. I. Sokolova, Valerie. II. Title.
BT367.F4B68 2011
226.7'09505—dc22
    [E]—dc   2010016479

Editor: *Mary Hassinger*
Art direction: *Jody Langley*

Printed in China

12 13 14 15 /DSC/ 10 9 8 7 6 5 4 3

Jesus Feeds the Five Thousand

story by Crystal Bowman
pictures by Valerie Sokolova

One day, a big crowd of people
was following Jesus.

Some of the people were sick.

They wanted Jesus
to make them better.
Other people just wanted to hear
Jesus talk about God.

Jesus wanted to be alone

with his twelve helpers.

He wanted to talk with them

and rest for a while.

So they got into a boat

and rowed away from the shore.

But the people ran along the shore

to stay close to Jesus.

Jesus and his helpers

rowed their boat back to shore.

They got out of the boat
and climbed up a hill.
The people climbed up the hill too,
so they could be with Jesus.

9

Jesus loved the people.

He wanted to help them.

So he stayed with them
and taught them many things.

After a while, it was getting late.

The people were tired and hungry.

Jesus asked his helper Philip,
"Where shall we buy bread
for the people to eat?"
Jesus said this to see
what Philip would say.
He already knew how
he was going to feed the people.

Philip said to Jesus,

"Even if we worked for eight months,

we could not earn enough money

to feed all of these people!"

15

Jesus had another helper

whose name was Andrew.

Andrew met a boy

who had some food.

Andrew brought the boy to Jesus.

"This boy has some food,"

said Andrew.

The boy had five small loaves of bread
and two small fish.

It was not enough food

to feed all the hungry people.

Jesus said to his helpers,

"Have all the people sit down."

There was a lot of grass

where the people could sit.

So all of the people sat down.

There were about 5,000 men.

There were also many

women and children.

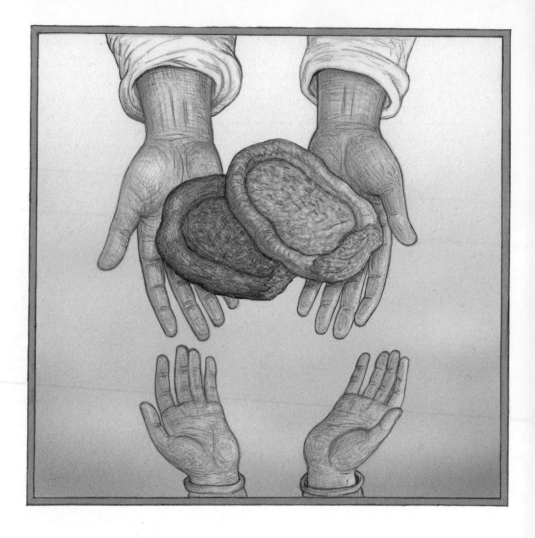

Jesus took the loaves of bread
in his hands.

He said a prayer to God
to thank him for the bread.

He asked God to bless the bread.

Then Jesus broke the bread

into pieces.

He gave it to the people.

As Jesus passed out the bread,

there was more and more bread.

The people could have as much

as they wanted!

Jesus did the same thing with the fish.

He asked God to bless the fish.

Then he broke it into pieces
and gave it to the people.

There was so much fish
that the people could not eat it all!
The people ate and ate
until they were full.

Then Jesus said to his helpers,

"Pick up all the food that is left.

Do not let any food be wasted."

So they picked up all the food

that was on the ground.

There was enough food left over

to fill twelve big baskets.

The people were very surprised!

"How did Jesus feed so many people?"

they asked.

"All he had were two small fish

and five small loaves of bread.

Jesus must be a special prophet!"

31

Jesus did many more great things

while he lived on Earth.

Soon the people knew

that Jesus could do great things

because he was the Son of God.